Animal

Lisa Trumbauer

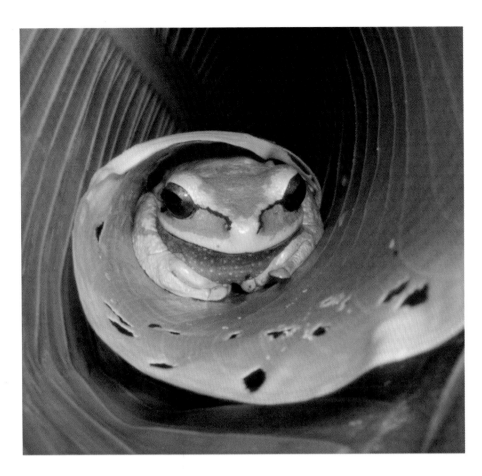

A frog is hiding
in a leaf.

A fish is hiding
in the reef.

A bear is hiding
in a cave.

A fawn is hiding
in the shade.

A duck is hiding
in the reeds.

A snake is hiding
in the weeds.

Who is hiding in this tree?
Look and look
and you will see.